SH*T

GIRLS

SAY

SH*T GIRLS SAY

KYLE HUMPHREY and GRAYDON SHEPPARD

First published in Great Britain by
Fourth Estate
a division of HarperCollinsPublishers
77–85 Fulham Palace Road
London W6 8JB
www.4thestate.co.uk
First published in the US and Canada by Harlequin 2012

A catalogue record for this book is available from the British Library

ISBN 978-0-00-749780-5

Printed in Spain by Graficas Estella

We dedicate this book to our mothers, sisters, grandmothers, aunts, and nieces.

FRIENDS
&
FASHION

What are you doing this weekend?

FROM STRANGER TO EX

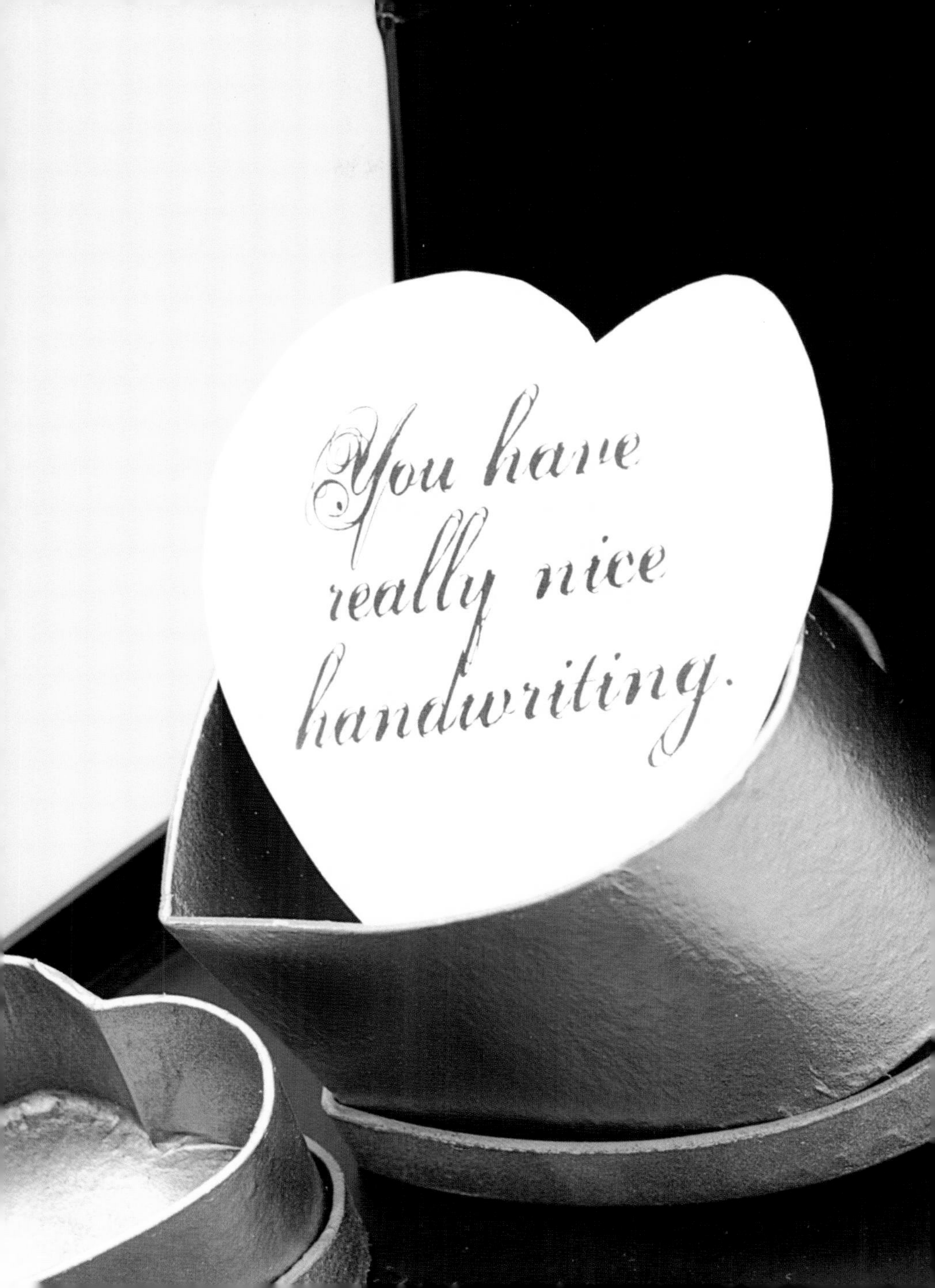
You have
really nice
handwriting.

Hey, where are you?
Did you miss me?
I'm excited for our date this week!
Was I super annoying last night?
My phone's being stupid.
Your phone must be off.
Are we in a fight?

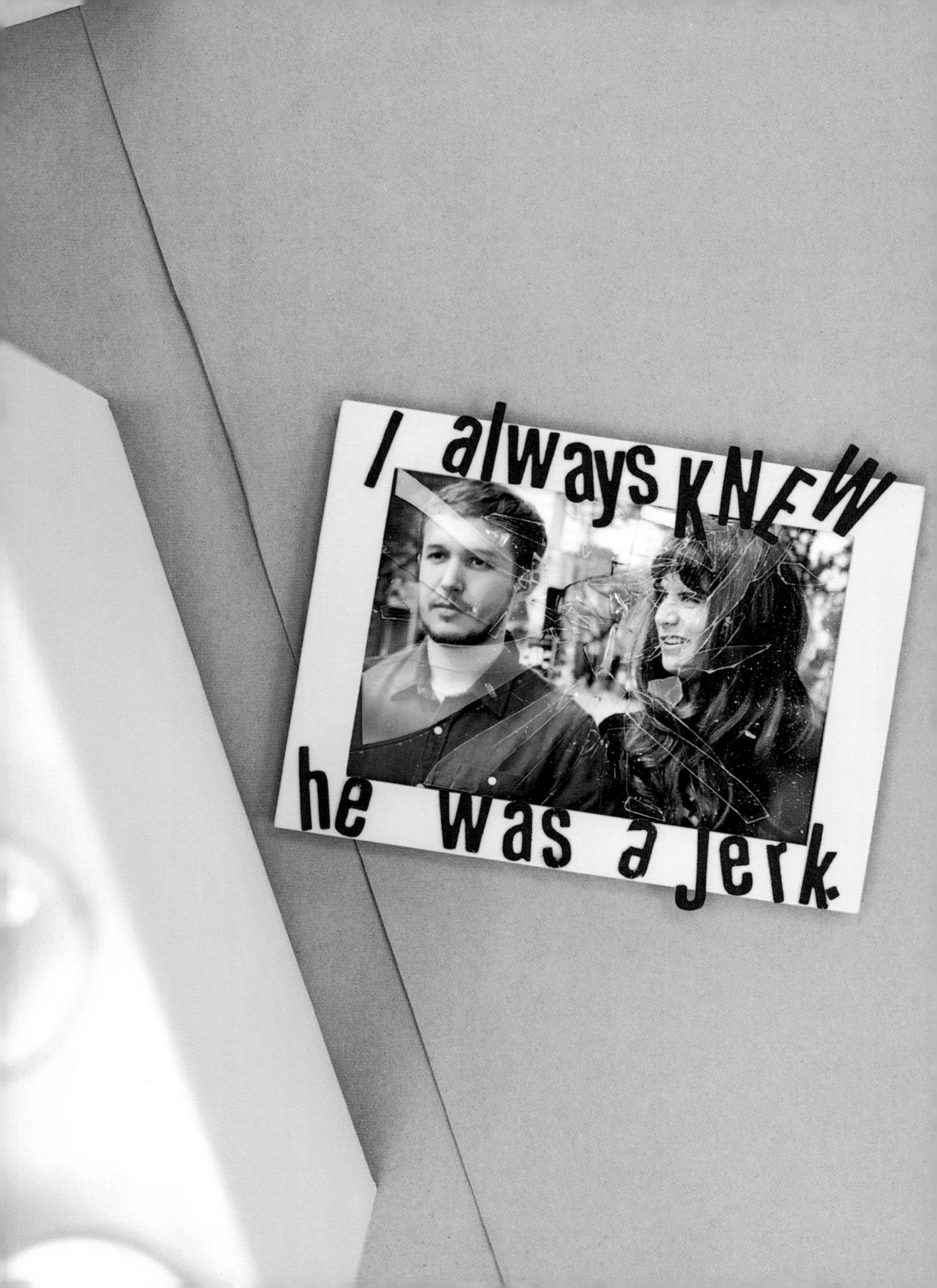
I always KNEW
he was a jerk

BODY ISSUES

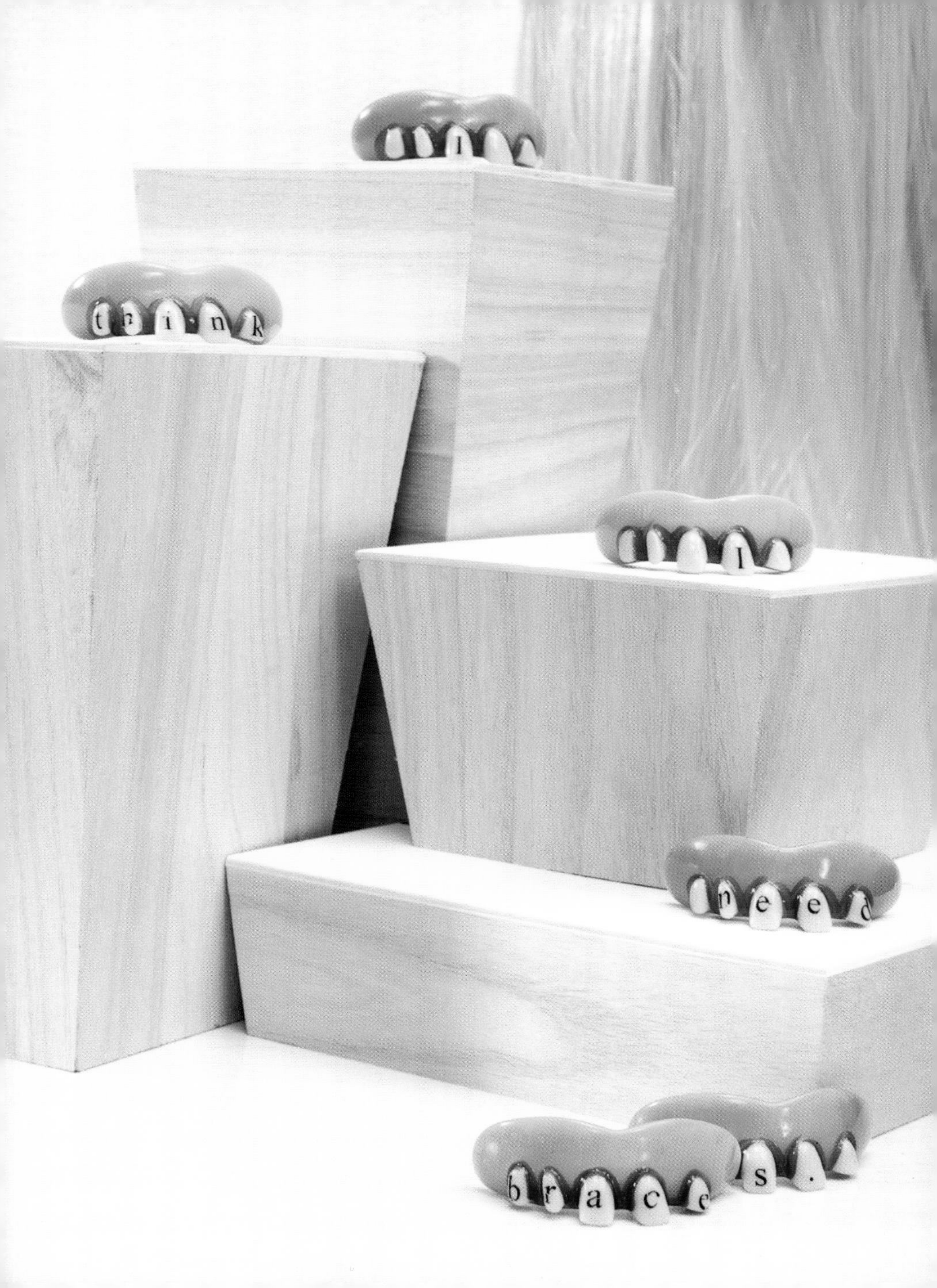
I
think
l
need
braces.

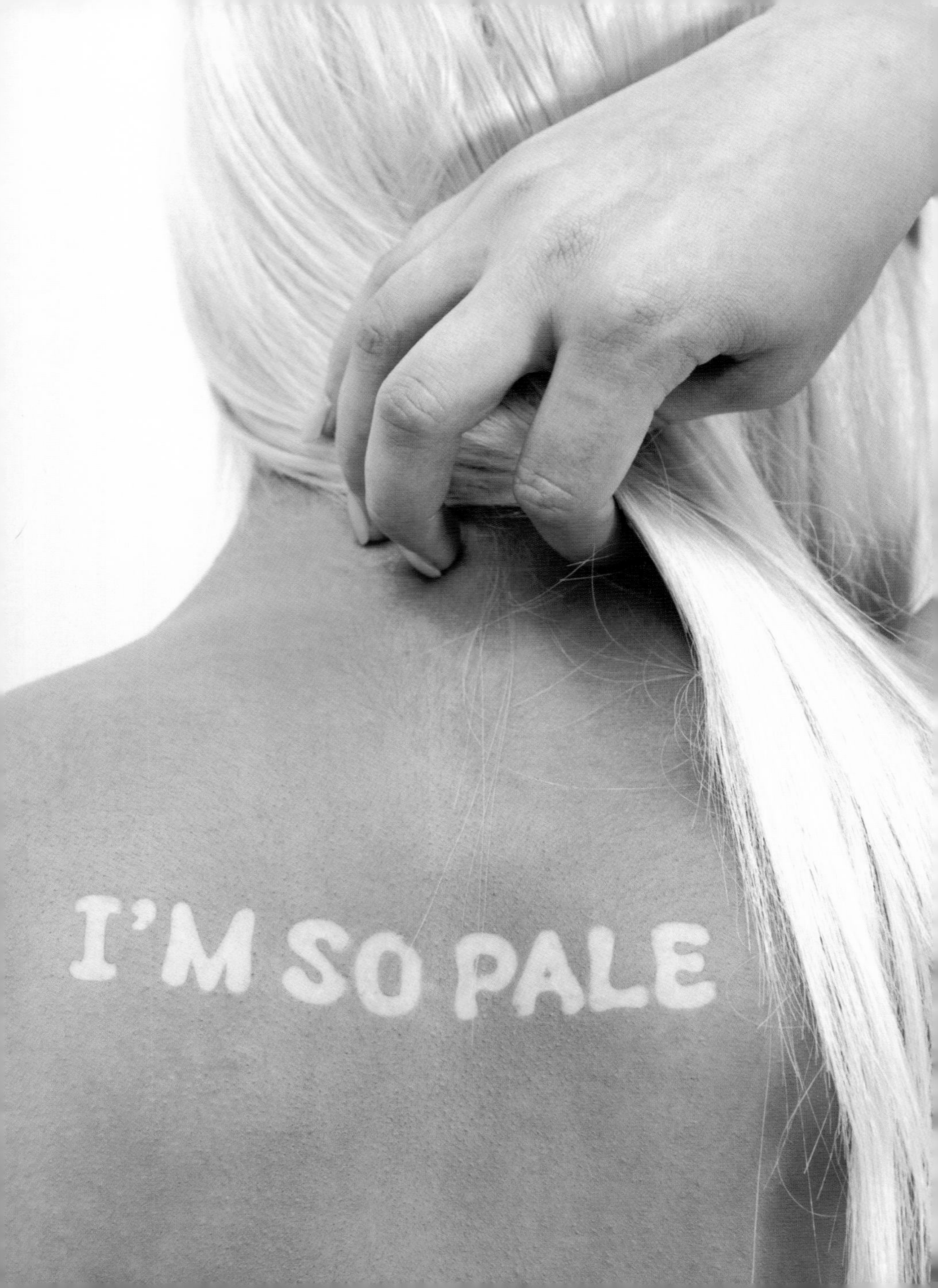
I'M SO PALE

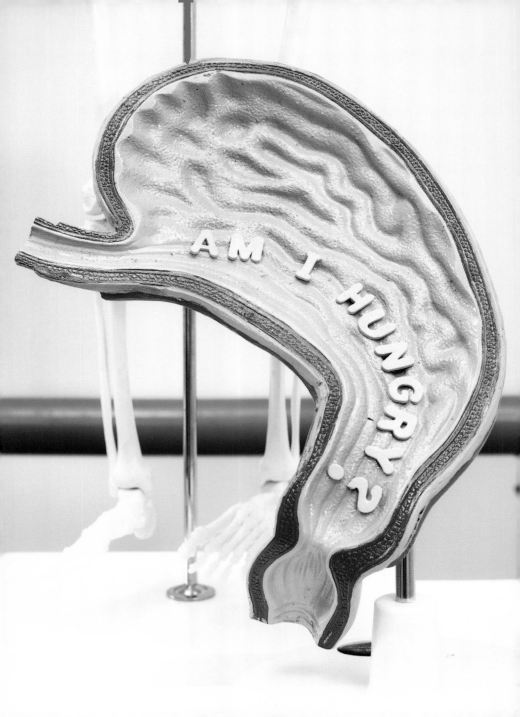

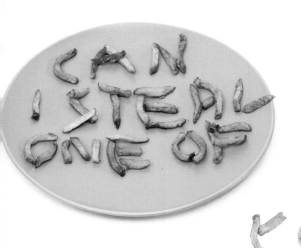

ALL THAT

I HOPE I'M NOT

GETTING SICK.

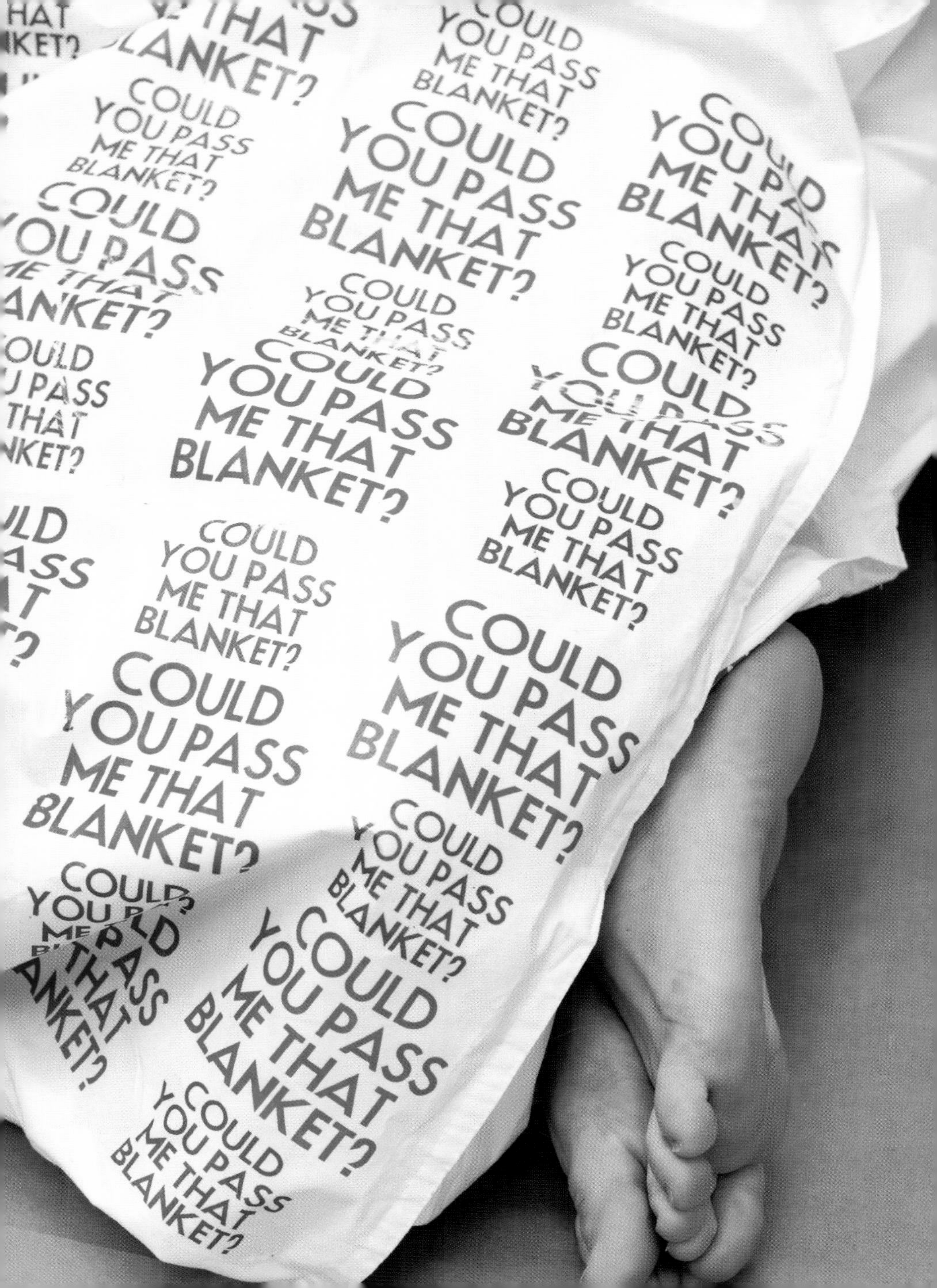
COULD YOU PASS ME THAT BLANKET?

SMALL
TALK AT
THE
PARTY

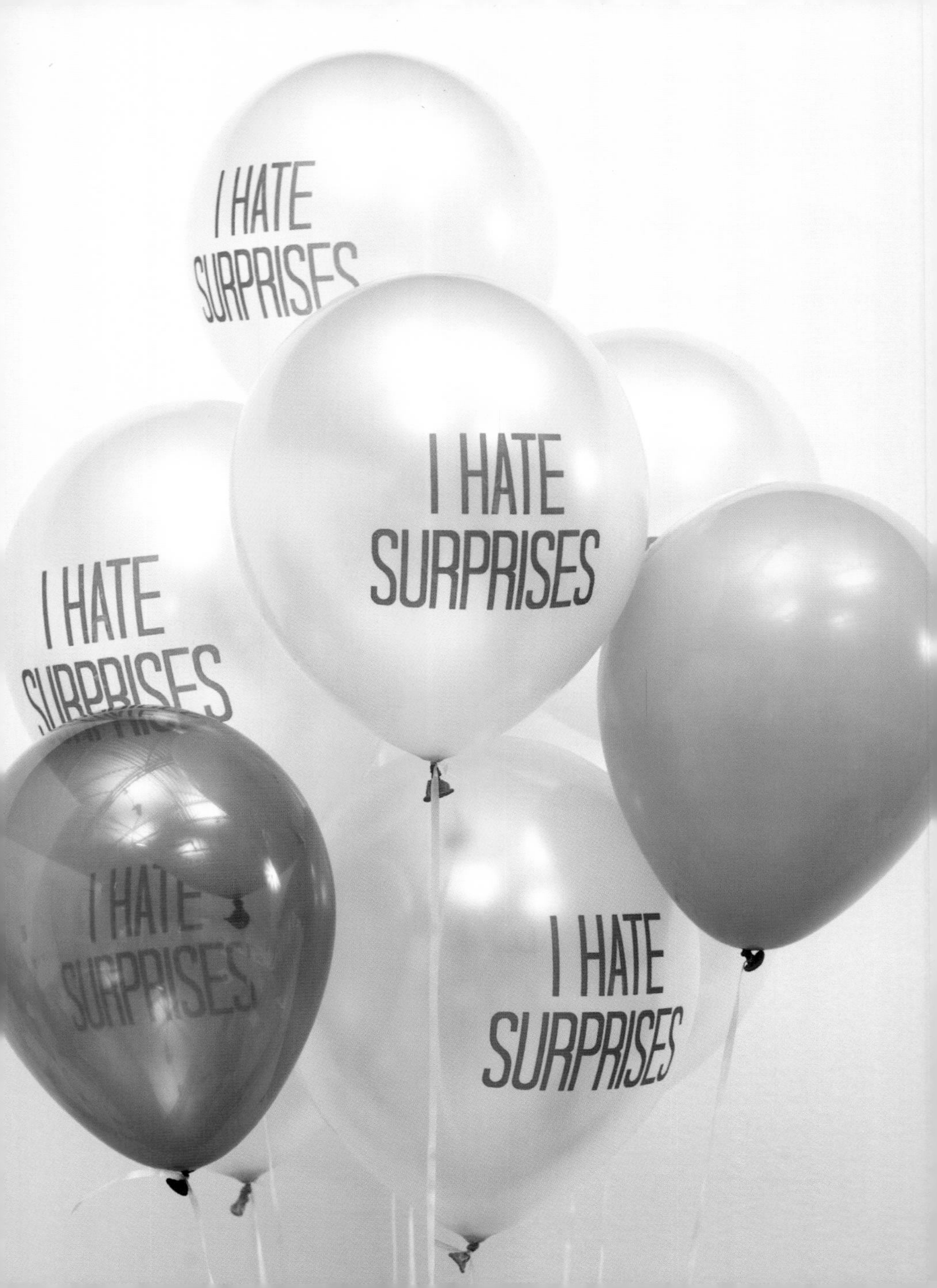

What if we did a bake sale?

WHAT'S YOUR
DOG'S NAME?

I'M TERRIBLE
WITH NAMES.

I'll have
a glass of
prosecco.

EMOTIONS
&
INSECURITIES

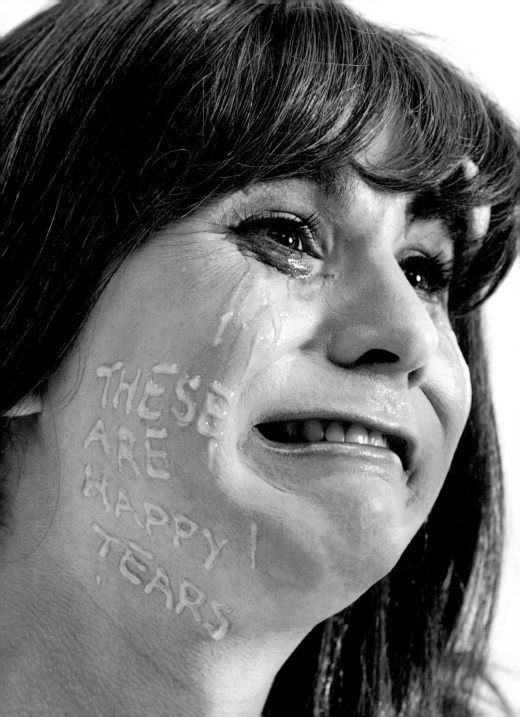

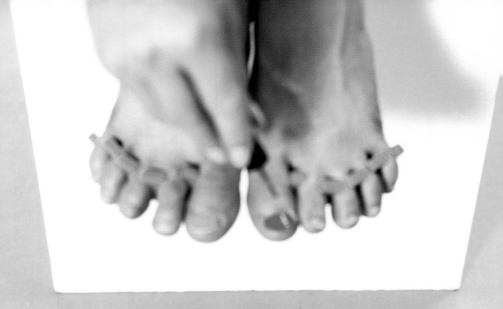

I wish I had time to meditate.

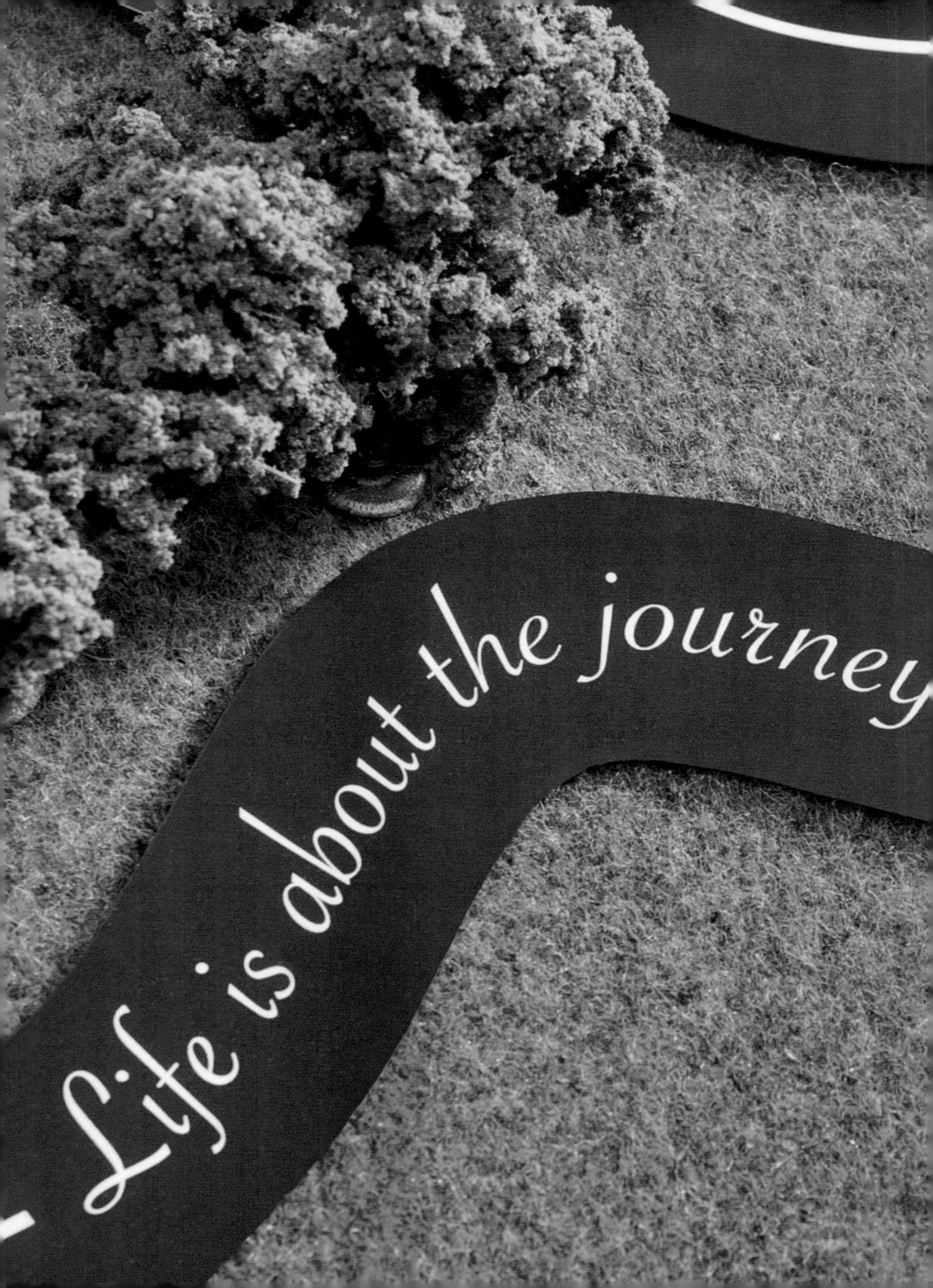
Life is about the journey

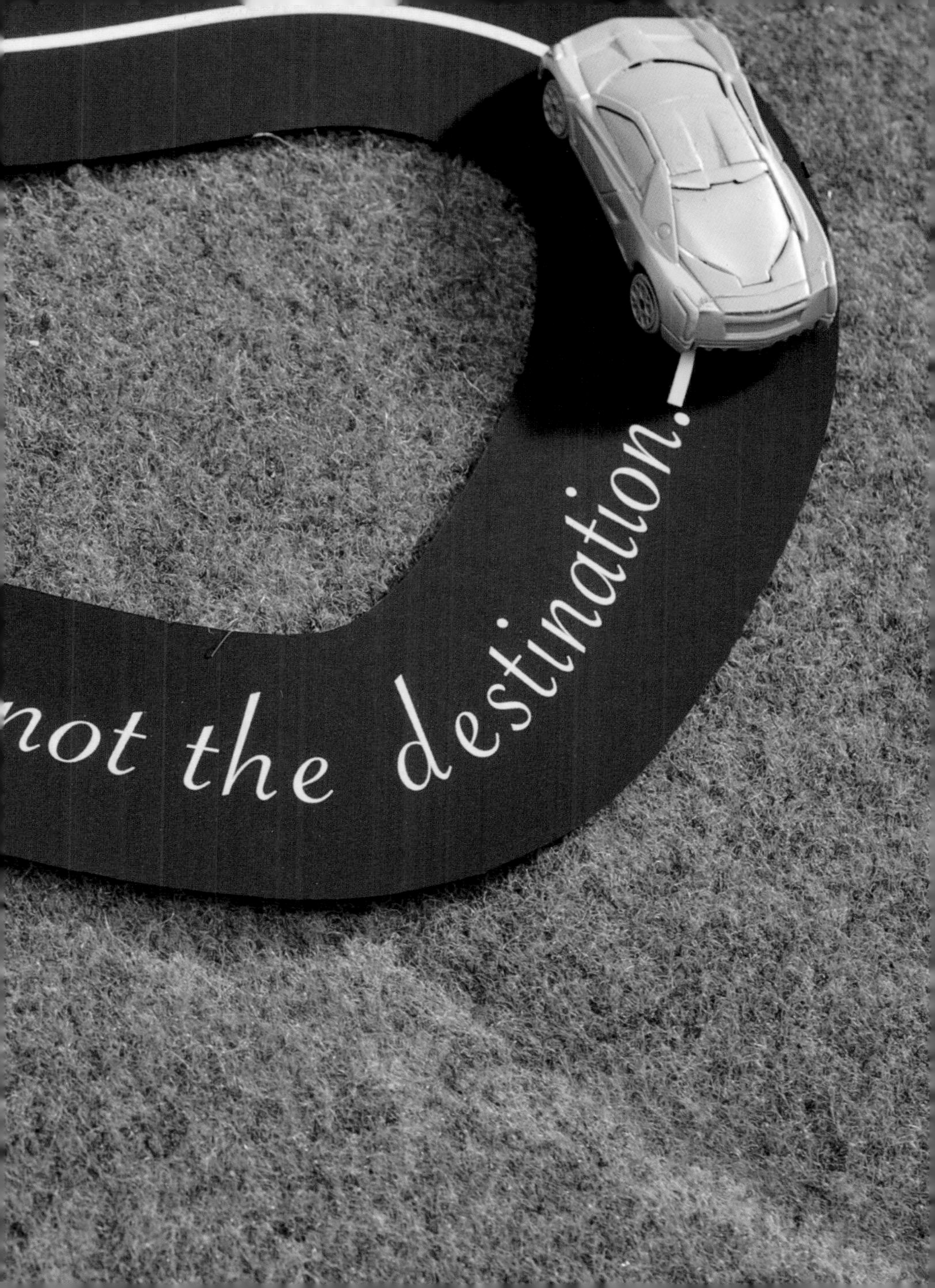
not the destination.

Photographer
Daniel Ehrenworth
www.dephoto.org

Photographer's Assistants
Joseph Devitt Tremblay
Matthew Tammaro
John Packman

Makeup & Hair
Robert Weir

Makeup Assistants
Meaghan Bell Gregory
Kelley Cloney

Wardrobe
Corrina Allen

Art Direction, Prop Styling & Graphic Design
Kyle Humphrey
Graydon Sheppard

Kyle would like to thank:

Madison, Mom, Dad, Gummy, Gumpy,
Grandma Marge and Grandpa Helge

Graydon would like to thank:

Gramma, Mom, Dad, John, Andrew and Cindy,
Kristen and Robert, Laura and Scott,
Maeve, Lila, Will and Cole

We would like to thank:

Deb Brody,
Simon Green, Emma Thaler, and the CAA team,
Shara Alexander, Jessica Rosenberg, Maria Ribas,
Sandra Valentine, Natasa Hatsios, Gigi Lau, Margie Miller,
Amy Jones, Debbie Soares, Nicki Kommit, Larissa Walker,
Arina Kharlamova, Reka Rubin, Christine Tsai,
Donna Hayes, Loriana Sacilotto, Craig Swinwood,
Brent Lewis, Alex Osuszek, and the Harlequin team,
Michael Lasker, Brent Lilley, Justin Letter,
Ryan Pastorek, Gregg Gellman,
Kirsten Nichols, Pamela Hamilton,
Sioban Quigley, Beaux Lewis-Quigley,
Margot Arakelian, Charlotte Glynn,
Christian Buer, David Chang, Ann Cockfield,
Juliette Lewis, Stacy London, Abby Elliott,
Ali Adler, Michael Ian Black, Jiffy Wild

About the Authors

Kyle Humphrey is a graphic designer, visual artist, and writer.

Graydon Sheppard is a writer, director, and the star of *Shit Girls Say*.

Kyle and Graydon are the co-creators of *Shit Girls Say*, which started as a Twitter account in 2011 and evolved into a viral YouTube sensation later that year. The videos have garnered over 30 million views.

www.kyledavidlarsenhumphrey.com
www.graydonsheppard.com

www.ShitGirlsSay.com